Praise for Ian Fee and
WILD RIDE TO SOBRIETY

"Ian Fee takes readers through his transformative life story in one wild ride—the power of sobriety is conveyed with such grace! His book is a must read for anyone who's sober curious."

—Maureen Evelyn, Maureen's Marketing

"In *Wild Ride To Sobriety*, Ian Fee takes readers on a restorative journey, offering a roadmap to healing and serenity. High praise for Fee and his honest, vulnerable, and matter-of-fact account of life in addiction and the beauty beyond it."

—Angie Ferguson, MS, PT, Author,
Speaker, Entrepreneur, and Coach

"As someone who works daily with people in recovery, I can attest to the importance of voices like Fee's in breaking down stigmas and showing that a sober life can be rich, fulfilling, and even exhilarating. This book is a must-read for anyone struggling with addiction or seeking to understand its grip."

—Rob Best, Founder & CEO,
The Barbell Saves Project

"It makes me emotional thinking about who Ian has become on his path to sobriety. The old Ian was running from life: His drinking and all nighters were part of this escape. Sober Ian is running toward ALL the life there is to live. I loved him then and I love him now, but this Ian is one I'm really proud of."

— *Nancy Everroad*

"Ian is a brother from another mother...Seeing him transform from shock and awe with family and friends to leading and lifting is a true inspiration!"

— *Tim Everroad*

"Ian Fee shatters the myth that sobriety is boring. He proves that a life without alcohol can be rich, fun, exciting, and deeply rewarding."

— *Matt Croak, Owner, Wise F&I*

"Ian is living proof that sobriety doesn't have to suck. Watching him live every day with a newfound purpose and reason has been amazingly fun to watch and be a part of. I couldn't be more honored to have a mentor like him in my life."

— *Nikkie Fee*

"I met Ian a little over a month after he got sober, and from the day I met him he's made an amazing effort to become a better man. His perseverance amazes me daily and I'm honored to have him in my life."

— *Shelby Johnson*

"*Wild Ride To Sobriety* isn't just a memoir, it's a roadmap for how to rediscover joy, purpose, and authentic connections with everyone around to you. Ian's book thoughtfully lays out a path for those looking to see what life can be like without alcohol and highlights the many gifts that follow."

—*Ryan Hoff*

"Ian inspires me to be a better person, and I celebrate his success! He has blessed me with the gift of knowing that nothing is out of reach when you aspire for greatness."

—*Bernie Radochonski, CEO/Owner,*
United Car Care

"Ian Fee's raw and honest account proves that the path to sobriety, while challenging, leads to a life more vibrant and fulfilling than any altered state can provide."

—*Dan Wilder, Jr., Wilder Auto Group*

"In *Wild Ride To Sobriety*, Ian Fee offers hope and practical insights for anyone questioning the role alcohol plays in their life."

—*Joel Olsen, Owner, Walla Walla Chrysler*
Dodge Jeep Ram

Wild Ride To Sobriety

WILD RIDE TO SOBRIETY

A Transformation
from Drunken Oblivion
to Profound Clarity

IAN FEE

Make It Great Publishing
Lynnwood, WA

Wild Ride To Sobriety:
A Transformation from Drunken Oblivion to Profound Clarity
© 2024 by Ian Fee. All rights reserved.

Published in the United States of America
by Make It Great Publishing

ISBN 979-8-9912237-0-6 (paperback)
ISBN 979-8-9912237-1-3 (eBook)

Ian Fee is available for speaking engagements.
Please email ian@wildridetosobriety.com.

For bulk discounts, contact ian@wildridetosobriety.com.

Cover and interior design by AuthorImprints
Author photograph by Emerson Fee

Manufactured in the United States of America

To myself—
The man I was, the man I became,
and the man I aspire to be

Contents

1

How I Puked My Way Out of My Alcohol Addiction

I CHECKED INTO SCHICK Shadel Hospital in Seattle for intense alcohol aversion therapy on October 20, 2017. I heard that aversion therapy had a 68% success rate, which gave me a much better chance at beating my addiction than the 8–12% success rate attributed to traditional rehab.

A friend and client of mine underwent aversion therapy a year before I did, after he and his wife kept getting into booze-driven jealousy fights. He told me it was intense and horrible—but it works. The fact that he was able to save his marriage, improve his relationship with his kids, and keep his multi-million-dollar business was all the inspiration I needed at the time.

I knew it would be a nightmare, but I was motivated to see it through to the bitter end. Looking back, I can't even believe I made it out alive, but when I was in the thick of it I stayed focused and never thought beyond the next five or ten minutes.

I'll forever be grateful to the nurses, counselors, hypnotherapists, and all the other people in the facility who got me and the rest of my cohort through to the other side. Everyone there was phenomenal, and I knew they were truly there to help me and make me as comfortable as possible.

Every other day, for 10 days, a nurse took me to what they called the Duffy Room. Before each of these appointments, I had to drink a two-liter bottle of blue PowerAde for the electrolytes (I have an aversion to that now, too!). Then they put me in a room with a single chair, a table, a silver bowl, a pink bucket, and a rag.

First, they gave me about a quart of ipecac, which is normally used to induce vomiting after ingesting certain types of poison. After that, I drank 16 ounces of warm salt water to make the ipecac work faster. Then the real fun began. One of the nurses (we called them bartenders for fun) gave me a shot of alcohol, which I had to swish around in my mouth for 30 seconds before spitting it out into the silver bowl. Then I did it again with another spirit. And again.

By the third shot, I was puking violently into the bucket and wiping vomit off my face with the rag. Only 15 more shots to go.

It took about 45 minutes to complete all 18 shots, followed by several hours of constant puking. By the end of it I was wrecked, but they made me take some ipecac again just to make sure everything was out of my system.

On alternating days, to recover from the non-stop puking, an anesthesiologist came in to sedate me with propofol, while someone else started asking me 26 personal questions. Things like who's your biggest influence, what helps you not drink, what's your favorite time of day to drink, where do you drink, do you think drinking in high school affected you today, did your parents abuse alcohol, etc. I didn't really know what I was saying as I drifted out of consciousness, but that was the whole point—they wanted the answers to come out reflexively.

After I regained consciousness, they took me for a personal counseling session. The psychologist revealed the answers I gave while sedated, and we started connecting the dots between my alcoholism and my personal traumas.

After repeating this cycle for 10 days, I was a free man. I wasn't tempted by alcohol in the least, even when I got my wife's divorce papers the day I returned home from the hospital.

While there wasn't anything I could do about the past, I knew that I could shape the future. I vowed to get through the divorce clean and sober and be a better dad, friend, and person going forward.

2

Bottled Deceptions

IT WAS 8:00 A.M. on day three of a company retreat, and I was a hungover wreck at the podium in the front of the large conference room.

Nausea churned in my gut as sweat drenched my back. Just four hours earlier, a colleague and I killed the last drops of a two-bottle wine nightcap back in my room—after closing the hotel bar.

A few minutes into my sales presentation, I paused to ask, "Hey, how much time do I have left?"

"Twenty-five minutes!" someone hollered.

Mustering a wry grin, I replied, "Perfect, because I'm gonna hurl in twenty-seven minutes."

The crowd of about 200, most fighting hang-overs as brutal as mine, erupted in laughter and cheers. They respected the hell out of my tongue-in-cheek confession, and my ability to power through no matter how miserable I felt.

During my time at the podium, and many years before and after I gave that speech, I really believed that drinking was the key to my success. Alcohol helped me forge valuable connections, seal lucrative deals, and celebrate life's victories. From spring breaks and office parties to client wining and dining, every occasion was an excuse to let loose and turn up the heat with alcohol-fueled shenanigans. And boy, did I push the limits.

I reveled in the glory of drunken escapades, not caring about the consequences. Passing out in strange places, hooking up with random strangers, and causing mayhem became the norm. I felt like I was really living because the party never ended. It was an everyday occurrence, from grabbing lunchtime drinks to indulging in Happy Hour after work.

Drinking was a sign that you had made it in my world. The more you could handle, the more prestigious you became. It was a never-ending cycle of pushing boundaries and seeking validation through excessive alcohol consumption.

Little did I know, while I was lost in a drinking bubble of my own making, that I was missing out on what truly mattered. The anxiety, the missed moments with loved ones, the toll it was taking on my mind, body, and soul—it all eluded me. I thought I was in control, but in reality I was a slave to the bottle.

It took a monumental crash for me to finally realize that I had it all wrong. Money and success came at a tremendous cost, and I was paying with my sanity, my health, and my relationships. The drama I caused and the apologies I had to make all ultimately culminated in a wake-up call I couldn't ignore.

As I reflect on my journey to sobriety, I feel the need to share my story with you. Not to boast about my triumphs, but to inspire and guide you on your own path to freedom from alcohol. In this quick read, I'll candidly share my personal experiences and stories from friends of mine who have battled their own demons successfully, too.

My hope is that amidst these tales, you'll find something that resonates. Whether it's a story that hits too close to home or a solution that sparks a change within, I want this book to be a beacon of hope and transformation for you.

I won't sugarcoat it—getting sober is tough. But if someone like me, who was written off as a lost cause, can do it so can you. The rewards of sobriety are immeasurable. I became a better parent, a better partner, and a better friend. I rediscovered the joy of living without the haze of alcohol clouding my every move.

So join me on this wild ride towards self-discovery and liberation. Together, we can burst that drinking bubble you're in and embrace a life worth living. And who knows, maybe your story will inspire someone else to make a change, too.

3

Sampling Sobriety

THE LAST THING I want to do is force sobriety on anyone, but I do love it when people use me as a role model. When people come to me for advice, I tell them to give sobriety a year and see what life is like without alcohol. See what your brain is like without it. And your relationships. All the booze in the world will be waiting for you if you ever decide to go back, but if you can give it a full year you probably won't want to.

And if you can't commit to a year right away, try a season. Or a month. Or a week, a day, an hour. However long you can stretch yourself will really make a difference. And whenever you feel yourself start to weaken, remind yourself how bad drinking is for you. That should at least buy you a little more time, and another chance to get it right.

It took me more than 40 years to choose complete sobriety, so I know it isn't easy. But the reason I wanted to share my sobriety success with you and others through this book is because it really does feel wonderful!

4

My Drinking Indoctrination

ALCOHOL ENSNARED ME BEFORE I even had a chance, its grip tightening from my very first breaths. My idyllic Bellingham, Washington childhood belied a drunkard's paradise, teeming with enablers. Our upper middle-class home was party central, a booze oasis where responsible parenting went to die.

I grew up yearning to join the inebriated inner circle of cool adults. Drinking defined our clan's bonding rituals, cementing it as the ultimate rite of passage. Long before I was legally allowed, alcohol was the anointed pathway to peer approval and adult privileges.

I became a prodigy, studying the masters at every raucous gathering. Generous grownups would knowingly encourage me to sample their libations as some stamp of misguided mentorship.

The photo below captures it all: my proud dad pouring beer down my mouth before my first birthday. It was a foreshadowing of much more to come.

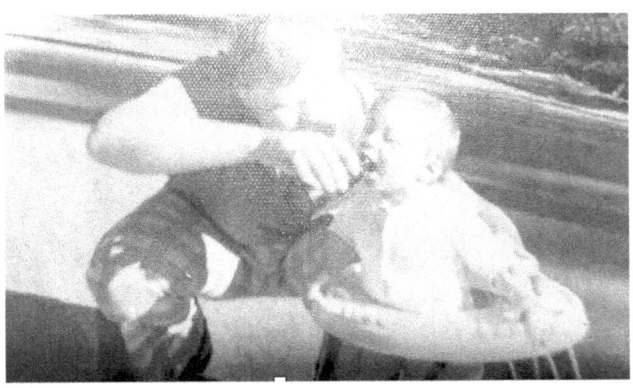

Baby's first beer! My dad encouraged my love of alcohol at a VERY young age.

By the time I was 10 years old, enabling had become outright encouragement. I remember the shock on other diners' faces when my parents let me sip the foam off their beer at a pizza joint. After the servers told them to stop and they didn't, we were kicked out amidst a cloud of sideways glances. In my family's distorted reality, it was simply the next phase of initiation into a culture where alcoholism masqueraded as bonding.

From my first memories, alcohol had its hooks in me and blinded me to its potential dangers. I was conditioned to believe it was an indelible source of joy, celebration, and upward mobility. For a long time, I remained oblivious to the fact that excessive drinking plagued my parents, their friends, and other family members. Although I observed the aftermath of heavy drinking, I failed to connect it to the euphoria experienced during the festivities.

5

The Armpit of the World

JUST BEFORE I TURNED 13, my world flipped upside down. My father received an exciting job offer to sell homes at a luxurious resort destination near Palm Springs called The Salton Sea. The Colorado River had breached a canal headgate, creating a beautiful lake that promised all kinds of family fun.

We packed up our belongings with enthusiasm, eager for the fresh opportunities but quite unprepared for the brutal desert heat. Those oven-baked temperatures were a rude awakening, but we had no idea an even bigger issue was bubbling up beneath the surface. The beautiful lake that drew us in was steadily becoming poisoned by salt, and the contamination would soon poison our promising new life.

Word spread quickly about the lake's demise, and people began abandoning the area in droves. Within months, my father's company went bankrupt, shattering his dreams and nearly leaving us homeless. We went from feeling on top of the world to teetering on the edge of financial ruin.

My father eventually found work as an accountant at a local agricultural firm, but his spirit was broken. He succumbed to a sense of victimhood, seeking solace in alcohol alongside my mother. Drinking became their only comfort, a desperate attempt to numb the pain of a world that seemed to have forsaken them.

When I was 14 or 15, I started washing dishes and stocking coolers at a local bar/restaurant called Johnson's Landing. All the locals and weekenders would hang out there after a long day of riding in the desert or boating on the lake, sharing drunken stories over frosted mugs of cold beer. Alcohol was around me everywhere I went.

6

You Call this Taking Care of Yourself?

WHEN I WAS 41, I found myself in the middle of a month-long bender, unaware of the toll the poison I kept consuming was taking on my body. It wasn't until I was peeing out blood one night at a bar that I realized there might be a problem.

Rather than seek immediate medical attention, I confided in the drinking buddy I was with. He advised me to continue drinking and deal with it later. At the time, it seemed like a reasonable suggestion.

When I finally saw my doctor, he informed me that my bladder was reacting like eyes do when they get bloodshot from booze. He told me to cut back on drinking and lose weight. I interpreted his advice as a suggestion to slightly modify my alcohol intake rather than make significant changes.

I proudly announced to my friends that I needed to take care of myself, limiting my beer intake from 16 to 12, shots from six to four, and 2:00 a.m. tacos from four to only three. They looked at me with pity as they indulged in high-calorie foods and empty-calorie alcohol while I "held back."

My doctor also informed me that vodka had the fewest calories. Naturally, I started consuming vodka sodas in large quantities, convinced I was making a healthy choice.

7

Cunning, Baffling, and Powerful

CO-FOUNDER OF ALCOHOLICS ANONYMOUS (AA), Bill Wilson, aka Bill W., described alcohol as "cunning, baffling, and powerful." He understood the destructive force of addiction firsthand, as it had sabotaged his own life on numerous occasions. He even lost a fortune by breaking a contract he signed with an employer, in which he agreed to quit drinking. He thought the huge financial incentive would keep him sober, but he only lasted three months.

Bill W. once said to an audience, "Some of you people may ask, why do these drunks continue to drink in the face of certain destruction—why can't they stop?" After all, it seems like such an obvious thing to do.

For people addicted to alcohol, however, quitting is an almost insurmountable task. The easier choice is to continue drinking, succumbing to alcohol's seductive grip. Even when you know alcohol is doing terrible things to you, like it was doing to me in my 20s, 30s, and 40s, you keep putting it into your mouth.

Alcohol was deep in my roots. It was difficult to shake even when I knew I was destroying my life and the lives of those around me to varying degrees of severity. Most people can get through the typical high school and college experiments with alcohol relatively unscathed, but for me—and about 11% of the U.S. population—that was just the beginning.

According to the National Institute on Alcohol Abuse and Alcoholism, 10.6% of individuals in the United States—29.5 million people—have an Alcohol Use Disorder (AUD). These numbers cut across gender, race, and ethnicity, indicating that alcohol addiction knows no boundaries:

- 16.6 million males (12.1%)
- 13.0 million females (9.1%)
- 18.7 million white Americans (11.0%)
- 5.1 million Hispanic/Latino Americans (10.3%)
- 3.5 million black Americans (10.1%)
- 982,000 Asian Americans (6.0%)
- 790,000 people of two or more races (14.7%)
- 280,000 American Indian/Alaska Native people (15.6%)
- 144,000 Native Hawaiian/Pacific Islander people (14.0%)

Most of these people will have to learn the hard way to break free from alcohol—if they're lucky. Many will waste their lives and others will die. Some will try to get help and relapse. It doesn't matter what their circumstances are, why they started drinking, or what they think they're getting from it, they're literally in a struggle for their lives.

Bill W. often said that drinking wasn't a habit, it was an obsession—an obsession that convinces us something external can fix what's broken within us. His own traumatic experiences, including abandonment by his parents at age 10 and the death of his first girlfriend at age 17, drove him to seek solace in alcohol. "The whole face of the universe instantly changed," he said about the time he took his first drink. "It released me from myself."

I'm very aware of the numbing effect of alcohol and other addictions, like drugs, gambling, and pornography. These vices allow people to temporarily escape the underlying issues that plague them. And people keep coming back to their addictions because the underlying cause never gets fully resolved.

The lure of alcohol is so strong, I've heard that even Bill W. asked for it at the end of his life. I'm sure he had his reasons, and I don't know if his request was even fulfilled. It just goes to show you that alcohol is not only cunning, baffling, and powerful, it's incredibly patient as well.

8

Working Hard—My Foundation for Hard Partying

AMIDST THE CHAOS OF The Salton Sea, I found solace in hard work at Johnson's Landing and other places in town. I thrived on earning money and observing the dynamics of success, driven by the fear of reliving my father's experience. To contribute to the family finances and establish my independence, I took on a lot of different odd jobs, from washing dishes and cleaning yards, to washing trailers and serving food and drinks for tips at parties.

I felt good about myself, and I enjoyed socializing with co-workers and customers. I soon learned that I was pretty good at schmoozing.

High school was also going well for me because I excelled in sports, earning accolades as the starting quarterback, point guard, and shortstop. Although I dabbled in drinking here and there in my teens, I managed to avoid excessive alcohol consumption and steered clear of drugs.

At home, however, the cracks in my family life were becoming apparent. My parents and I lived together in a state of detached coexistence, resembling roommates more than a traditional family unit. Communication about important matters never happened, and their absence from my sporting events spoke volumes. I had to mature quickly, lacking the emotional support and nurturing that a normal childhood should entail.

9

I Hated Getting Drunk—the First Time

SUMMERS IN HIGH SCHOOL provided a welcome escape from the Armpit of the World. I got to return to Washington to spend time with my college-age brothers and childhood friends. I would stay with my parents' best drinking buddies, once again immersing myself in the familiar party scene of my earlier years.

The summer after my junior year in high school, I experienced my first true drunken initiation while visiting one of my brothers at Washington State University. After pounding way too many cheap beers, I vividly remember puking all over the brand-new Air Jordans I'd spent months saving for.

I was extremely pissed off, as you'd expect any 17-year-old to be, but the nightmarish incident had a silver lining: it kept me away from booze for a little while longer. Unlike Bill W., my first experience with alcohol didn't release me from myself, it released me from another $125 to replace the shoes.

10

Poolside Living

AFTER GRADUATING HIGH SCHOOL in 1990, I took my dad's advice and skipped the university route. Instead, I jumped straight into the working world. While my athletic talents could have secured me a full scholarship at a decent school, I lacked the guidance to navigate the college admissions process.

So instead of hitting the books, I purchased a modest travel trailer and relocated to Indio, California, the "big city" just north of The Salton Sea.

I landed a gig as a pool attendant at a swanky Marriott resort in Palm Desert. In many ways, it was the best job I ever had: I got to spend my days basking in the presence of gorgeous, bikini-clad women all day long. And when my shifts ended, the real fun began as we pooled our tips and partied into the early morning hours.

II

My Downward Spiral

MY POOLSIDE JOB AT Marriott piqued my curiosity about hotel management. I moved to Chula Vista with my high school sweetheart, enrolled in a vocational program, and took a construction job to pay the bills.

It was during this period that my drinking took a darker turn. After catching my girlfriend in a compromising situation with a sketchy, tattooed neighbor, I spiraled into a world of seriously heavy drinking to cope with the heartbreak. Following in my father's footsteps, I adopted a sad "woe-is-me" mentality and stupidly sought comfort at the bottom of a bottle with my friends.

I moved in with a buddy of mine in El Cajon, and that's when my drinking ramped up into truly reckless territory. We embarked on nonstop benders, with cases of Mickey's Big Mouths stashed in my truck. We even converted my washer fluid reservoir into a mobile vodka dispenser, adding the intoxicating elixir to various

Big Gulps. Alcohol saturated every aspect of our daily existence.

Despite my growing recklessness, however, I managed to stay committed to my vocational studies. I even landed a front desk position at a downtown San Diego Holiday Inn, and that's where the unholy marriage between work and alcohol became permanently ingrained. Every night after clocking out, my colleagues and I went full-tilt into the party-boy lifestyle. My routine rarely varied: classes from 9:00 a.m. to 2:00 p.m., work from 3:00 p.m. to 10:00 p.m., then girls, bonfires, and enough alcohol to drown a small town.

12

Weak Losers Don't Drink

IN MY WARPED MIND back then, when I was fueling my career with alcohol, the poor souls who suffered the devastating wrath of liquor's punishing effects were just weak losers who couldn't keep up with winners like me. I'd watch colleagues flame out, resign from work, move to different cities, or fade off into the sunset because they just couldn't handle their liquor like the cool kids.

And, like they say, out of sight out of mind. Shortly after these people left and traces of their transgressions were swept under the rug, those who remained drank a toast to them and kept the party raging on.

I had convinced myself that excessive drinking was a prerequisite for career success. High-roller clients loved getting wined and dined to the nines. And, when I advanced far enough in my career to be the one doing the wining and dining, I loved providing them with over-the-top experiences they couldn't get anywhere else. My efforts were rewarded with lucrative contracts time and time again.

As a keen observer of human behavior, I noticed that the ability to order an expensive bottle of wine at the finest restaurants was the mark of true professional success. I also discovered that, at the executive level, your liquid courage earned you a free pass to be absent from all the grunt work. All you had to do was show clients a wild time while your underlings kept things going (and cleaned up your boozy messes).

You might have to swoop in for some occasional crisis management or critical executive decision, but if you had the instincts you could usually wing it. And even if you crashed and burned, corporate never seemed to care. The unspoken code was that high-level executives were expected to keep their partying just on the edge of out-of-control. The culture pushed you to drink to your limit, but it was up to you where that line was drawn. No one gave you a playbook.

Most people in my experience managed to walk that tightrope without any serious fallout like financial ruin or jail time. But those who blew it had to take their show on the road, so us kings could keep reigning supreme.

13

A Bright Spot? Your Network Is Your Net Worth

MY ABILITY TO CONNECT with people on a deep level served me well during my wild early years. I'm a very social, extroverted person and I loved being around friends in class, at work, and out on the town raising hell. Three of my mentors when I was in my late teens, two former high school teachers and a vocational instructor, really drove home the importance of networking and fostering great relationships by taking care of people and making them feel great.

It came naturally to me. My mom always stressed that it's better to give than receive, and that making other people happy is one of the most important things you can do in life. She could whip up a huge party with friends in no time. Both my parents were social dynamos, and I often wonder how things might have turned out if they had a different circle of friends in Washington and didn't get derailed by the disaster in California.

I quickly learned how easy it is to build a solid network—socially and professionally—just by showing appreciation to people, even in little ways. Since most people don't make any effort in this simple area, you can really stand out just by asking about someone's interests, remembering details about their family members (especially spouses and kids), and giving thoughtful gifts related to their favorite indulgences on special occasions—or just because! To this day, even though I'm solidly sober, I still surprise clients with their preferred wine or spirits just to brighten their day.

Alcohol seduced me by becoming intertwined with fun times and profitable relationships. As a young man in my twenties, raking in good money and being the life of the party every day made me feel like I was on top of the world.

Little did I know that my unsustainable, party-hard lifestyle was planting the seeds of a catastrophic, two-decade spiral that would jeopardize my health and alienate me from the people I loved most.

14

The Wives Were Out for Me

BACK IN MY PARTY animal days, I loved playing the benevolent leader role and rewarding my employees. This often meant buying rounds after work. Happy Hours routinely turned into four- or five-hour marathons before anyone realized it. My guys never made it home to their families at a decent hour.

The wives of my crew hated me for being such a toxic influence, keeping their husbands out boozing until last call. Those poor women were powerless to stop their men from going full bender with the boss, and they had to deal with the aftermath of the drunken escapades. The whole dynamic wreaked havoc on their marriages, all in the name of professional development.

Today, these same wives appreciate me—and some of them adore me—because I actively encourage my guys to be present husbands and fathers. The people in my orbit saw me turn my own life around in a dramatic way, and they've become healthier because I'm no longer a bad influence.

15

My Drinking Bubble

MOST PEOPLE WHO DRINK don't even notice that they're not aware. When I was an alcoholic, I lived in a drinking bubble. Sure I felt the hangovers, but they went away—even quicker if I started drinking early the next day and looked forward to the next happy hour.

What I didn't feel was all the anxiety that drinking was causing me, because it never left. In fact, I absorbed the anxiousness so completely that I couldn't even remember what life was like without it, even if I wanted to. The funny thing was, I thought I was in complete control when I was totally out of control.

The devil was always on my shoulder, tempting me away from what was truly important in my life, like my wives and kids—you know, those buzzkills and inconveniences who interfered with my quest to get ahead and provide for them!

I had to work! I had to bring home the bacon! I HAD to keep drinking at a frenzied pace so my clients would love me and throw more business my way. I had to keep up with my bosses and show my crew a good time when it was my turn at the top. That's how the world worked for guys on the fast track to success.

Do I regret how I lived my life up to this point? Not really, because I was a victim of circumstance. Do I wish things had worked out differently? Sure. I made money, but it came at an unbelievably high cost. I'm not proud of all the drama I caused. And I'm truly sorry about missing time with my kids that I can never get back.

16

Who Cares What People Think?

PEOPLE ON THE OUTSIDE looking in at my boozy bubble would give me all kinds of flak (and talk behind my back) about my alleged "alcohol abuse," rowdy antics, and trainwreck of a lifestyle, but I didn't listen. Their nagging protests just went in one ear and out the other and I felt sorry for them for not enjoying life.

I honestly didn't realize I had a problem with alcohol for the longest time. I mean, I knew on some intellectual level that overdoing the sauce could be hazardous. But only for the lightweights who couldn't hold their liquor like a crafty veteran partier such as myself.

I was performing at the highest levels while partying with the best of them. Blacking out here and there was just the price of admission to keep soaring with the big dogs.

Those puritanical buzz-killers just didn't get it. What did they know about cutting loose and chasing the ultimate rush? Their shrill scolding only reaffirmed that I was doing something right, living my truth as a renegade while they clung to their boring, sober snoczefests.

17

Inklings of Sobriety

THE FIRST PERSON I ever met who gave up drinking and got completely sober was a 24-year-old guy named Tim. He remains one of my true inspirations and has become a close, lifelong friend.

Back when he was coaching my son's basketball team he was a fun person to hang out with, but our drinking often led to chaotic situations. One memorable incident involved him throwing up on my floor and attempting to clean it up with my vacuum. It was a disgusting mess.

Tim's wake-up call came when he was stopped by the police on the freeway. He wasn't in a car—he was walking! Realizing that his excessive drinking made him a danger to himself and others, he made the decision right then and there to never touch alcohol again. He could have been roadkill!

Reflecting on stories like Tim's can serve as a reminder of alcohol's destructive power and how it can bring out the worst in people, leaving a trail of chaos and regret in its wake.

As historian Tom White aptly stated, for those addicted to alcohol, limiting themselves to just two drinks is an impossible feat. After the first drink, the guy or gal making the decisions is already a different person.

18

Money Can't Buy Your Presence

BACK WHEN I WAS getting my career going and climbing the corporate and entrepreneurial success ladders, I deluded myself into thinking that my wives and kids wanted for nothing because I was bringing home the bacon. As long as I kept the cash flowing, they could buy whatever their hearts desired and be the envy of all their friends.

What I failed to grasp was that my loved ones weren't pining for more material excess. No, what they desperately craved was the presence of a normal, engaged husband and father who was willing to prioritize quality family time over the relentless pursuit of wealth and debauchery.

I was too preoccupied chasing the superficial trappings of success to notice that the people closest to me were sitting at home, missing me and wishing for me to just be there with them. My family would have gladly taken a pay cut if it meant being able to spend more time together. But I was tragically blind to the fact that they mattered more than any fat paycheck ever could.

19

Alcohol Chooses You

A GOOD FRIEND OF mine, a fellow former party animal who has joined me on the journey to sobriety, has an interesting theory: you don't choose alcohol, it chooses you. And once it's embedded itself in your life, you and everyone around you start subconsciously making all sorts of deranged adaptations to accommodate its overpowering presence.

You might catch yourself making ridiculous rationalizations like, "Chardonnay makes me angry so I switched to reds and I feel so much better...But I had to get my teeth whitened to deal with all the wine stains."

Or, if your boss is a raging lunchtime lush who turns into a holy terror after knocking back a few too many, you learn to just steer clear and not engage with him after noon.

My friend thinks alcohol has such a vice grip because people would rather contort their lives into psychological pretzels than confront the elephant in the room—their unacceptable behavior—and seek the help they really need.

I have a lot of experience in this regard, but one example stands out in my mind. One year I was watching the Masters golf tournament at Hector's Restaurant in Kirkland, Washington with my buddy Johnny. We sat there for breakfast sipping mimosas, ordered beers with lunch, and switched to red wine for dinner. We drank non-stop the entire day without ever leaving the place, and my wife had to pick us up after our nine-hour drinking escapade.

20

Turn it off and on Again

I ALWAYS MARVELED AT one buddy of mine's ability to stop drinking whenever he wanted to. He could amazingly go years at a stretch without touching a drop. One of his funnier stories involves his never consuming alcohol throughout his first marriage, only for his ex-wife to spot him at a bar with drink in hand shortly after their divorce. "If I knew you drank, I might have stayed with you," she remarked with a laugh.

While my friend could oddly turn that faucet off, it was just as easy for him to crank it back on at full blast. Like me, he was hardwired for alcohol from day one. It was embedded in the DNA of his family, built up through years of extravagant parties, daily cocktail hours at home, and family fights. In good times and in bad, alcohol was a bonding experience that became pervasive in his household, like it has in so many others.

And that's the insidious thing: because alcohol is so connected to both celebratory and emotionally traumatic occasions—the highs and lows of life—it becomes easy to use excessive drinking as a maladaption to all kinds of extreme situations.

For my friend, drinking excessively to show his success was motivated in large part by his father's saying he'd never amount to anything. He wanted desperately to prove his dad wrong. But even when my friend finally "made it," his dad accused him of being a criminal.

21

Self-Medicating the Wounds Within

I'D ARGUE THAT ANYONE who hasn't experienced some form of deep-seated trauma is probably not a heavy drinker. Organizations like AA have a very specific structure for a reason: in the fight against addiction, most people need to peel back the layers of anxiety, pain, dysfunctional patterns, and emotional turmoil that initially drove them to escape reality through substance abuse.

AA's pioneering 12-step program provides a systematic framework for members to work through their core issues. By admitting powerlessness over their addictions, taking a moral inventory of themselves, making amends, and ultimately achieving a spiritual awakening, recovering alcoholics who go through the program confront their demons head-on. Members are also encouraged to work closely with a sponsor who has worked the steps himself or herself, providing experienced mentorship throughout the process.

Perhaps most importantly, AA meetings foster a culture of fellowship, where members share their personal stories of addiction's destruction and ultimately redemption. This communal sharing can help some people shatter the feelings of isolation and shame that so often compound an alcoholic's suffering in silence.

Although I've never attended or felt the desire to attend AA or any other 12-step program, they definitely have their place in the world of recovery. But if they don't work for you, take heart that many other agencies, resources, and tools are out there to help.

I believe that addictions fundamentally mess with our moral compass and our ability to make good choices. Not only do we stray when we consciously indulge an addiction, but once we're under its spell the further we get from our true, inner selves. It doesn't matter if the addiction is alcohol, porn, caffeine, vaping, diet fads, sugar, shopping, exercise, or anything else: any of them can consume us when taken to an unhealthy extreme—even the so-called "good" ones.

Relying on addictions as Band-Aids for difficult situations merely masks our real underlying problems, while slowly corroding our spirits that desperately yearn for healing and relief. We ignore the fragmented parts of ourselves in dire need of acceptance and care when we numb them with addictive behavior. And that's the tragic, insidious power that addictions carry— the ability to destroy us from the inside out, tainting our most precious relationships and sapping our life force.

Now that I better understand how alcohol was symptomatic of deeper mental health struggles, I often tell people there's an underlying reason they can't put down the bottle...and it's got absolutely nothing to do with the taste of alcohol.

22

The Worst Addiction

ALCOHOL IS ONE OF the most destructive addictions out there, because it doesn't just ravage the addict—it lays waste to every life surrounding him or her, too. Other vices like cigarettes might be turbo-charged cancer delivery systems, but at least their fallout is generally limited to the user.

Alcohol's collateral damage radius is far more expansive. It turns good people into strangers: loving husbands become abusive monsters, devoted mothers start neglecting their kids, and responsible workers derail into unemployable liabilities. All from a mind-altering toxin that's legal and socially accepted.

The alcoholic becomes a black hole at the center of their universe, violently pulling in and disfiguring every valuable relationship, every meaningful priority, every scrap of goodness within their orbit. Families are shattered, futures are squandered, and souls are irreparably tarnished.

And the true heart of the tragedy? The addict is often the last to realize the full extent of the path of destruction they've blazed, the countless bridges they've burned through complacent negligence. That's the malignant, traumatic power of alcoholism.

23

The Cupcake Analogy

A GUY I KNOW uses the cupcake analogy to illustrate how many people dismiss alcohol as a problem. Imagine this description of a long weekend:

"Well, I started eating cupcakes on Friday afternoon, and continued eating them until about

Midnight. I probably had about eight cupcakes on Saturday during the day, plus a few more at dinner. After that we went out and ate cupcakes all night long. Brunch on Sunday was just as insane—bottomless cupcakes!"

If someone said this to you, you'd think they had a serious problem. But if they say "drinks" instead of "cupcakes," lots of people think it's cool.

24

Happy Hours—and Hours and Hours

A SUPPOSEDLY QUICK HAPPY hour with the boys after a hard day's work would invariably transform into a night-devouring bender spanning three, four, or sometimes even five aimless bar-hopping hours.

By the time I finally staggered back home from these escapades, reeking of booze with a whiskey headache already blossoming, any semblance of quality family time had been squandered away. Dinners missed. Hellos and goodnights slurred in passing as little feet shuffled off to bed. Countless Monopoly games and homework help sessions unfulfilled.

While the sting of shame would flare up with each morning's light, the disappointing cycle kept repeating in my pursuit of professional success.

In the haze of those selfish years, I was willfully, utterly clueless to the conflict slowly calcifying between my two loves, the bottle and my own offspring. One all-consuming infatuation guaranteed the other's perpetual, heartbreaking abandonment.

Now long since faced, that colossal dereliction of fatherly duty during such fleeting, formative years will forever remain my heaviest cross to bear. My selfishness robbed my children of emotional riches that no amount of Future Me's regret can ever bring back.

25

Couch Cushion Coin Hustles

NOTHING COULD STOP ME from getting alcohol. At one point, my financial situation was so dire that my wife and I would conduct fullblown scavenger hunts around the house on the weekends, flipping couch cushions and scouring under car seats. We'd collect all the change we could find to afford one measly box of swill wine for $6.99.

26

Settling into Alcoholic Life

BY THE TIME I got married and had my first kid in 1995, I was hitting the booze hard. I was working at a hotel in Seattle, and I partied with my boss and crew all the time while my poor wife handled our newborn solo.

My nightly bro-fest camaraderie scored me a steady stream of promotions. I became the hotel's chief money man—the CFO calling the fiscal shots. And, in my other role as Night Manager, I was in charge of running the hotel bar before I could even legally buy a beer. That pretty much gave this raging alcoholic the keys to the candy shop.

My career was an unstoppable supernova of success when kid number two arrived in the summer of 1997. But instead of dialing back the party lifestyle, I doubled down to keep the growing family gravy train chugging.

Justifying my perpetual drunken absence by providing for the family protected me from seeing what I was really doing to myself and the people around me.

27

Drunken Side-Gig Shenanigans

ON TOP OF MY regular job, I was running a side hustle mowing lawns and landscaping with one of my drinking buddies on the weekends. We drank at bars more than we worked on lawns, but we had a realtor friend funneling us a steady stream of older, affluent clients in our town's ritzier neighborhoods.

We weren't the best landscapers, but we excelled at client appreciation. Our clients loved us for the constant barrage of thank-you cards, flower bouquets, Easter baskets, Valentine's Day treats, and other gifts I would bring them.

By taking those extra steps to brighten my clients' days with thoughtful little gestures, I forged real connections that transcended my amateur landscaping abilities.

In an age of impersonal, automated customer service, people are starved for genuine care and recognition. A simple handwritten note or an inexpensive knick-knack can sometimes mean more to someone than all the expensive, sleek professionalism in the world. Those early experiences breaking through to clients on a personal level showed me the unexpected dividends that can come from making people feel genuinely valued and appreciated as human beings first and clients second.

28

Booze, Boats, and Bad Decisions

WHEN MY KIDS WERE about four and six years old, I embarked on a new career in the automotive business as a finance manager at a car dealership. My new boss was best friends with my old boss at the hotel, so the nightly benders, booze-cruising jaunts, and incessant partying picked up right where it left off.

After a couple years, the car business started wearing thin on my home life. I bailed for a General Manager role at a Howard Johnsons, but that just made things worse. I ended up having a torrid affair with my sales manager there, nuking my first marriage for good.

During that tumultuous time, a warranty rep I knew floated a straight commission business partnership my way. I had always wanted to go into business for myself, so I figured it was worth a shot. Freshly divorced and scrambling to keep my kids fed, however, I racked up $35K in credit card debt that first year, while only taking home eight grand in the same timeframe. To save money, I moved in with my friend from the landscape business, which led to a bunch of hot-tubbing ragers fueled by cheap whiskey.

Things began to pick up in my second year in the automotive warranty business. Naturally, I attributed our new-found success to all the "client entertaining" we did, a thinly-veiled excuse for a rotating bacchanal of seedy strip clubs, alcohol fueled deep-sea fishing excursions, and reckless barhopping.

29

Egged on by My New Bride

DURING THAT CRAZY TIME, I fell in love again and got married for the second time in April 2003. But instead of becoming a stabilizing force, my new wife only emboldened my party lifestyle. With dollars rolling in at an accelerated pace, she actively encouraged me to keep squiring prospective whales out of productive "client entertaining" sessions.

From 2004 through 2016, our warranty business was an absolute gold mine. The money was coming in fast and furious, and we learned how we could use alcohol as a weapon as we were evaluating prospects. We'd bring people out for deluxe steak dinners or midday liquid lunches and listen intently as they regaled us with tales of their business prowess and vast corporate empires.

Meanwhile, our wives doubled as secret agents at the other end of the table, getting the real scoop from our prospects' wives. A few chardonnays later, the real tea came spilling out about how their husbands had too much on their plate, their companies were on the brink of bankruptcy, the kids were in rehab, etc.

30

Alcoholism Was My Superpower

IT MAY SOUND CRAZY, but I genuinely believed that drinking was one of my superpowers. I took pride in being able to keep up with, or even outdrink, my prospects, clients, colleagues, bosses, and subordinates known for their partying. Matching people drink-for-drink built rapport and social bonds. I had to be careful not to outpace certain people, however, if I sensed it would make them feel left out or inferior.

As juvenile, stereotypical, and sexist as it all was, with all the cringe-worthy golf outings, steak dinners, boating adventures, strip club debauchery, and conference shenanigans, the fact remained that the biggest deals we made were because of interactions centered around drinking. The people I attracted thought that if I was this wild and fun, they should do business with me so the party could continue forever. I built my career on alcohol-fueled experiences, so what could possibly be bad about it?

The more I was able to use people's vices to provide a WOW factor, by getting bottle service at a club or giving expensive booze and cigars as unexpected gifts, the deeper our bonds would grow and the more profitable our relationships would become. Depravity was a force multiplier, at least in my line of work.

31

A Frog in Boiling Water

WHILE ALCOHOL WAS PROPELLING my business success, it was also causing my personal life to gradually spiral out of control. I was like a frog in a pot of water slowly heading towards a boil, oblivious to the damage being done.

I failed to realize how I was neglecting and embarrassing my family. What may have been glorified behavior in my younger years appeared pathetic as I continued the same habits into my 30s and 40s.

I couldn't see the forest for the trees because alcohol poured itself into my personal life just as easily as it flowed in my professional life. Just like my parents did when I was little, I hosted plenty of "family-friendly" events where the kids ran around and played while the adults got blasted. I brought coolers filled with beers, mimosas, and bloody marys to my kids' sporting events, and at one point I even bought an RV that became a traveling party bus.

32

You Know it's Bad When...

A FRIEND OF MINE often met his wife for a drink after work. Nothing wrong with that, right? Well, on numerous occasions they'd have to leave their cars at the restaurant after one drink turned into four, five, six, etc.

One time, this happened repeatedly over a week's span. Each time they returned to retrieve their vehicles, they ended up getting drunk again instead of just driving away.

33

Sober Curious

ON OCCASION, ESPECIALLY AS I got older, my friends and I would talk about what it might be like to abstain from alcohol. For me, those thoughts were always fleeting because I just liked drinking too much.

I already told you about my friend who was able to go years at a time without drinking if he put his mind to it. He was the most sober curious of our group of raging alcoholics.

As the years went on, before he became completely sober like me, he would always give himself an exit strategy when we were engaged in alcohol-fueled client dinners and other business-related social activities. We called him Houdini because he'd often discreetly leave the party after contributing fully for a couple of hours. People usually didn't even realize he had gone.

While I was able to compartmentalize my drinking by going crazy at the parties and then functioning like it never happened during the workday, my friend always said he felt like he was driving with the emergency brake on at work whenever he was drinking regularly. He was moving, but not at top speed. He knew something was off, but he couldn't quite put his finger on it. That was the nagging feeling that always made him curious about what a sober lifestyle would be like: he knew on many levels that he was always happier and more productive during his dry spells.

34

My Last Hurrah

EVERYTHING SEEMED TO BE going great in my life until May 2017, when my second wife told me to quit drinking. She wasn't kidding. The extreme ups and downs of my crazy mood swings were really getting to her, and she was tired of constantly defending me to our kids.

Knowing that some of my buddies could quit cold turkey whenever they wanted, I did it too without a second thought. I wanted to save my marriage, and if that's what it took so be it. Despite my assent to her wishes, however, my wife and I kept getting more and more distant from each other.

In September that same year, at a Buffalo Bills game in New York, I drank for the first time since her ultimatum and kept going the entire weekend. I'm not going to lie, it was fun. Once again, my family was at home doing family stuff while I chose to party and be away from them. I rationalized it away because I was traveling with a good friend of mine, but that special occasion turned into another six weeks of heavy drinking.

Finally, on October 16, 2017, I had the last alcoholic drink I've ever had. It was to celebrate my son's 22nd birthday in his college town of Ellensburg, Washington. Just four days later, I checked myself into Schick Shadel Hospital in Seattle for the 10 days of fun I described in gory detail at the beginning of this book (see story number 1).

I came out of the program a new man on Halloween, only to be served divorce papers the same day—a sobering experience indeed!

While it was tempting to hit the bottle again, I couldn't have done it if I wanted to. Aversion therapy made alcohol completely repulsive to me. But even more than that, I wanted to have a clear head to try and save my relationship.

When my wife's uncle told me on November 22 at 5:05 p.m. that she was having a fling with her best friend's brother, however, I knew things were over between us. The news shook me to the core. I was mad at myself for all the drama I caused over the years and all the time I missed with my kids that I could never get back. I had to face the fact that I was a terrible husband and father.

35

Assessing the Damage

BEING A FUNCTIONAL ALCOHOLIC is a curse. You think you're fine for the longest time when you're really destroying yourself and ruining lives all around you. You blame everyone for your problems, except the only person who's responsible—you.

When I got out of Schick Shadel Hospital, I was forced to examine my life without alcohol's numbing effects. I had to look my life right in the eye and try to repair as much of the damage I'd done as I possibly could.

I'm grateful that I've been able to make amends with at least some of the people I dragged through Hell with me. And I work hard to earn and maintain the trust and love of my kids. I had to spend a lot of time apologizing to them, and I'm doing my best to make up for the lost time.

A close friend of mine, who recently quit drinking as well, is lucky enough to still have young children. He's been cherishing every moment with them now, making the most of the second chance he's been given.

While I was being honest with myself after rehab, I realized that the prospect of becoming an old drunk was another reason sobriety had an appeal for me. I had my turn at fun, and I was lucky that my genetics gave me the resilience to bounce back from all the physical abuse I put myself and my liver through. I was also lucky that my stupid antics didn't wind up killing me or anyone else, which could easily have happened anytime I was drinking and driving. So, when I really thought about it, I just didn't want to squander whatever remaining time I had left.

With a clear head, I realized that my lack of awareness kept me trapped in a prison guarded by alcohol. But after my aversion therapy I was free and could make a fresh start. Committing to being sober was scary on one level, but also incredibly exhilarating.

36

Find What Works for YOU

YOU'VE GOT A MILLION different ways to get on the path to sobriety. What worked for me may not work for you. (FYI, Schick Shadel Hospital closed its doors in June 2022, after 85 years of service.) We're all unique individuals, and I encourage you to try as many things as you can and keep searching until you find whatever works best.

AA is a great option for many, but if you think it's the only solution out there you'll be pleasantly surprised to find alternatives. And if you try something and fail, don't give up. Keep trying new approaches until you find what works.

I relied on a combination of techniques to free myself from alcohol. Some of these were easy for me, like gathering information about what alcohol addiction is and how it can be treated and talking to other people who've gone through it. Others were extremely difficult, like aversion therapy.

37

Sober Games

LOTS OF PEOPLE MAKE a game out of testing their ability to go sober, and that's a perfectly valid approach these days. Can you make it through Dry January or Sober October? How about One Year No Beer? No-alcohol challenges have become quite common and they're a good way to see how strong of a hold alcohol has on you.

Research shows that it takes 90 days for a habit to really stick. But even a few days without alcohol is better than nothing, and maybe if you can get through 30 days without drinking you'll keep going for 60 more on your own.

In many ways, these challenges take the pressure off by making sobriety fun or creating a little friendly competition, but people often go a little crazy once the challenges are over and can indulge in alcohol as a reward.

38

Mentors & Coaches: Invaluable Assets

IN ADDITION TO MY closest friends, I've turned to therapists, life coaches, and mentors to hold me accountable and keep me on track with my sobriety, my personal life, and my professional life.

Two life coaches over the years have taught me some powerful self-improvement techniques, like daily journaling, refusing to take on other peoples' problems, and writing down goals and breaking them down into small, attainable steps.

After I got sober, I didn't do everything all at once to change my life overnight. Instead, my healthy habits evolved gradually. Take cold showers, for example. It's an incredibly healthy morning ritual, but when I started I couldn't last 10 seconds. Now I get in for a minute or more and it's nothing, but it took many months to build up my endurance.

My current life coach, Angie, has been a tremendous blessing in my life. During our hourly check-ins every 10 days, we focus on various goals I've set—breaking them down into short (weekly), medium (90 days), and long-term (3-5 years) benchmarks.

For the longest time, I wanted to become a runner. Angie is an avid marathoner, and she's helping me stick to a training regimen to one day compete in a race.

If hiring a therapist or coach isn't feasible financially, seek out someone you admire as a mentor. Many people may jump at the chance to provide guidance—it never hurts to ask. Failing that, observe their behavior and emulate their habits. And of course, feel free to reach out to me anytime: my email is in the back of the book!

39

Recommended Reading

I ALWAYS SUPPLEMENT THE guidance I get from my friends, coaches, therapists, and mentors with motivational books from experts in health, medicine, business, relationships, and other important aspects of life.

My recommended reading list includes these great titles:

- *Atomic Habits* by James Clear
- *Good to Great* by Jim Collins
- *The Power of One More* by Ed Mylett
- *The Power of the Subconscious Mind* by Joseph Murphy
- *The School of Greatness* by Lewis Howes
- *The Untethered Soul* by Michael Singer

In addition to those, I'm going to single out two books that really had a profound impact on me.

The first one is *Principles for Success* by billionaire investor and hedge fund manager Ray Dalio. He lays it all on the line quite simply:

"You need to decide for yourself what to do and you need to have the courage to do it...Good decisions will reward you with good outcomes and bad decisions will hurt you."

Some people need this kind of brutal honesty to spark an important course correction, but then what? Dalio outlines a five-step processes for evolving to increasingly higher levels of success:

1. Know your goals
2. Identify and don't tolerate your problems
3. Diagnose your problems to get at their root causes
4. Design a plan to get around them
5. Implement your plan

You'll notice that four out of those five steps deal with obstacles that can get in the way of your path to personal victory. For me, alcohol was the problem that prevented me from achieving my most important goals of building loving relationships and self-respect.

Dalio recognizes that success is an ongoing process, and if you can get help from others who are strong where you are weak you can achieve great things. Dalio is a firm believer that it's not just okay to ask people for help, it's critical to break through the "Blind Spot Barrier" we all put up sometimes. "If you can look at things with the help of others who can see what you are blind to, you'll see much more than you can alone," he writes.

Two other related points in the book that continue to resonate with me include leaving your ego at the door and sharing your mission with people you can be "radically truthful and radically transparent" with. I couldn't have gotten sober without my closest friends, and I certainly couldn't have maintained my sobriety alone.

More great life advice comes from a book called *The Four Agreements* by Don Miguel Ruiz and Janet Mills. I first encountered this amazing book when I was getting my aversion therapy: the folks at Schick Shadel Hospital used it as the foundation for our group therapy discussions.

Based on ancient Toltec wisdom, the book explains how a powerful code of conduct can replace self-suffering with freedom, happiness, and love. All you have to do is faithfully follow these four simple rules:

1. Speak Impeccably
This agreement with yourself emphasizes the power of words and encourages speaking with integrity and avoiding gossip, judgment, and hurtful comments. The idea is to use language in the most truthful and kind way possible.

2. **Do Your Best**

This doesn't mean you have to be perfect or struggle—just do your reasonable best in any given situation without judging yourself harshly. By keeping this agreement, you can avoid self-punishment and regret.

3. **Don't Make Assumptions**

People often make assumptions about others' intentions or motivations without having all the facts. This agreement challenges you to ask questions and communicate clearly to avoid misunderstandings.

4. **Don't Take Anything Personally**

This agreement reminds us that when others judge, abuse, or try to diminish us, it's a projection of their own reality and emotional baggage. By not taking things personally, we avoid reacting with anger or hatred.

40

Reactions to My Sobriety

WHEN I REVEAL MY non-drinking status, re-actions run the gamut. Some who knew me as a lush think I'm putting them on. Others think I'm crazy for giving up alcohol's "wonderful" buzz. A few twisted souls want me to fail, letting them off the sobriety hook.

Then there are those who want to know how I did it, what it feels like, and if it bothers me be-ing around peole who drink. Many say nothing to me at first, only to circle back months or years later with profuse thanks for inspiring them to get on the sober path.

These folks may not have sworn off alcohol entirely, but they've cut down to the point where they might have a mixed drink or a glass of wine once a week instead of several drinks every night and more on the weekends. Regardless of the quantity of alcohol they've eliminated, they all say the same things about how much better they feel and how they have a whole different mindset when it comes to drinking.

41

Caught vs. Taught

OVER THE YEARS, I'VE learned we all become examples for others, whether we want to or not. This is especially true of parents to their children, and how I behaved in front of my kids when I was drinking was very damaging to them.

I really believe in the idea that you don't get to opt in when it comes to being an example to your children, or to anyone else for that matter: You either set a good example or a bad one.

This is especially important because things that are caught are internalized a lot more than things that are taught. I could tell my kids not to drink till I was blue in the face, but they saw me do it every day and that's the message they got. Actions speak louder than words.

My own parents' alcohol-fueled modeling undoubtedly shaped my behavior around drinking. While not an excuse, this awareness helps me check any misdirected anger towards my kids. The last thing I want to do is perpetuate generational patterns any more than I already have.

My greatest alcohol regrets revolve around time and experiences stolen from my children. I understand the subconscious damage inflicted and I'm diligently encouraging health and healing through daily actions. Remarkably, they've shown immense forgiveness as I strive to show them what a good father can be.

42

Letters from My Kids

WHEN I WAS GETTING ready to write this book, I asked my kids to send me a couple of short paragraphs about their memories of me as a dad. Specifically, I asked for a funny drinking story and some thoughts about something I did or didn't do that made a negative or positive impact on them.

My daughter Maddy, a policewoman whose courage makes me swell with fatherly pride, penned this letter about my journey from alcoholism to sobriety that drove home the "caught vs. taught" truth:

"My dad was gone a lot growing up. He was around for all the important things, but not the day-to-day stuff. It was never a normal upbringing in our house. The house was always full of people, drinking, and partying. I didn't know much different, so I never thought much of it. Often around dinner time I would ask, 'Where's dad?' The response was normally 'out to dinner/drinks with clients.' When he got home, we never really knew which dad we were going to get; the goofy fun one or the grouchy one.

"I knew he drank a lot, but it was all I ever knew so I didn't know it could be different. When he went to rehab and got sober our relationship changed significantly. We did so much together— walks, hikes, dinner, coffee, movies, etc. Stuff we never really did together before. I am so proud of the work he put in and the way he has showed up for his family, friends, and himself. I don't think our relationship would ever be the way it is now if he kept drinking, and I am forever grateful for his strength in getting sober."

My son Bailey, an assistant golf pro, also chose words that cut to the heart:

> "Funny Story: It was a football Sunday at the Brier house and you stayed in the hot tub for 12 consecutive hours, starting at 8:00 a.m. with a bloody mary. You then moved on to vodka sodas, then beer, then wine—never once getting out of the hot tub. Somebody was always making you a new drink or bringing you a plate of food: Yes, you ate breakfast, lunch, and dinner in the hot tub!
>
> "The memory that stuck with me is more of a compilation of things. When you reached a certain point you had zero filter, and I have different memories of some very vulgar/rude things that were said. Not to me specifically, but to other people: family, friends, neighbors. Don't get me wrong, you still 100% speak what's on your mind but when you were drinking it reached a different level."

My youngest daughter, Emerson, also shared her childhood memories:

"When my dad was drinking I was still very young but there are some things I still remember to this day, like always asking my mom, "Where's daddy?" She always said he was at work and promised he'd be home soon. Sometimes he made her look good by coming home shortly thereafter, but most of the time he stayed out for hours. We never knew. After a while, I figured out that he wasn't working in the middle of the night but was drinking and partying instead. He's a much better person—and dad—now that he doesn't drink."

It pains me to know I was absent for so much of my kids' childhoods because of my drinking. But I'm grateful for their honesty and that we now have open, loving relationships built on mutual understanding and respect. Getting sober has allowed me to be the present, engaged father they deserved all along.

43

A Kaleidoscope of Vibrant Life Changes

EMBRACING SOBRIETY HAS BROUGHT plenty of positive changes into my world, from the deepening of personal relationships to a rediscovery of purpose and passion.

After I quit drinking alcohol, I became a better father, partner, friend, and boss. I went from being a weekend warrior to a dedicated exerciser. And I have a much clearer head at the office, while still managing to have fun. I'm a much better role model to the people who work for me, and I'm much more content in my own skin.

It's not always easy to stay sober, and as a work in progress I'm constantly trying to improve myself and fight off temptations. I haven't given in because I've received endless gifts and rewards from putting down the bottle. Sobriety allows me to be my best self for family and friends, and that's what keeps me going.

These days, my goal as a proudly sober man is to positively impact at least one person daily. Family, friends, employees, service workers, strangers—anyone I encounter is eligible.

44

Fun with Hookers

NOT TOO LONG AGO, I was in a hotel lobby bar with my best friend—I wasn't drinking alcohol, of course, but he was—and we had the occasion to chat with two young ladies of the evening.

Impressed with their sales and entrepreneurial skills, we tried to redirect their energy for long-term success into careers they could really be proud of. I don't know if they took our advice to heart, but I'm sure their interaction with us was a run-in with some traveling businessmen they've never had before.

*It was always ok to sip on champagne
on special occasions.*

Fat in Vegas—Back then I was neither physically nor mentally healthy.

My parents had a special love for each other.

My first home purchase—Indio, California, 1990.

*My brothers—Bruce, Derrick, and Allan—with me
and our dad just a few months before he passed.*

My three kiddos with my parents in The Salton Sea.

My room at Seattle's Schick Shadel Hospital, where intense aversion therapy cured me of my alcohol addiction.

*Steve and Ryan are two of the most important
people in my circle. We drank together for
decades and now we're sober together. I
couldn't have done it without them!*

*Steve and his wife Diane have been incredible
sources of emotional support along this journey.*

*Joel and Julie have been with me since my
drunken days. Julie likes me better sober because
I don't keep her man out late anymore.*

*Mike and Lori have always been a huge source
of support for me—they're epic friends for life!*

I still have great times sober with my bestie Dane.

My ride or die best friends, Dane and Matt.

No conversation is off limits with my best friends in the world, Amy and Dane.

Celebrating my 50th birthday—and five years of sobriety—with my best friends in the whole world.

Dane with Emerson, my youngest, at The Salton Sea. The dead fish smell made him wonder if he was in Hell.

*The best part of being sober is being
present for my kids and my gal.*

*My love, Shelby, has never seen
me take a sip of alcohol.*

*I don't have to drink to have fun anymore. Here
I am at a concert with my daughter Maddy
and her best friend, my bonus kiddo Abby.*

*It's great to be emotionally present
as well as physically present.*

*My son Bailey and my daughter
Maddy with my mom.*

My purpose—the three best kids ever!

45

The Sober Body

ALCOHOL HAS A LOT of calories: About 600 in a bottle of wine and 800 in a six pack of beer. Every shot you throw down is another 100 calories. And mixed drinks are the real killers, with about 275 calories in a typical margarita.

When you drink to excess, the calories add up fast. And when you add in all the associated chips, dips, steaks, potatoes, late-night taco runs, and ice cream binges you can easily get a week's worth of your recommended calories in a day or two. I remember times when my weight would fluctuate 11 or 12 pounds—during a weekend!

As bad as you start to look on the outside from drinking excessively, what's going on inside is even worse. Alcohol consumption can lead to chronic illness and other serious problems, such as high blood pressure, heart disease, stroke, liver disease, digestive problems, and certain cancers.

Many of these same issues are compounded when you're overweight or obese, because then you have to worry about type 2 diabetes, sleep apnea, depression, and musculoskeletal conditions.

Quitting drinking initiated a dramatic physical transformation for me. Within four months, 55 pounds had melted away. I had a lot more energy. I was getting stronger. My skin looked healthier. My clothes got looser. And my friends, coworkers, and family members started to notice, too. The compliments about my new appearance and vigor kept on coming, providing a positive ego boost and fueling my commitment to a fitter, healthier lifestyle.

Today, I'm 84 pounds down from my peak drinking weight and I'm no longer on any medication for high blood pressure or anxiety. All my vitals are at peak performance.

Now when I go to the gym or go for a bike ride, I actually receive valuable health benefits instead of just sweating out booze. And choosing to eat more organic food and get more sleep is icing on the cake.

Not drinking has freed me up to focus on health, longevity, and extending the quality of my life as much as possible. I started out my journey of sobriety just wanting a clear head, but I got so much more—all the way down to my toes.

I'm exponentially happier, fitter, and more focused than that boozy former shell of myself could have ever imagined. And, years into sobriety, I can say with certainty that nothing good ever arose from drinking. It bred countless bad decisions that jeopardized my health, my life, and the lives of others.

46

All the Good Times Without the Hangovers

THE BEST THING ABOUT being sober is you can still have as much fun as everyone else and feel like a million bucks the next day.

You can still go out and socialize and be the life of the party if that's your nature. You can still go to concerts and comedy shows. You can still attend or participate in sporting events. You can still joke around and laugh at a bar with your friends. You can still have intense, philosophical conversations about the meaning of life. You can still have romantic dates and great sex. You can even drink—as long as there's no alcohol in your glass.

Then, while everyone else is hung over and feeling miserable the next morning, you're getting a workout in. Or you're spending time with your family. Or you're advancing your personal or professional life by reading a book like this one.

I sure don't miss missing days. While I was very resilient when I was younger, I pushed myself to the limit often enough that countless hours were squandered hungover on the couch, my passion and productivity utterly paralyzed.

47

Get Your Brain Back

DRINKING CREATED A LOT of unnecessary "noise" in my life that threw me off balance. Living a life of sobriety has given me my brain back so I can better handle life's curve balls.

When you've been sober for a while, you start to see things more clearly. Your highs and lows aren't as exaggerated, and you can make better decisions based on facts instead of emotions.

You can also be there for other people in a more positive way. From a sober vantage point, it's easy to notice when other people are struggling through some of the same things you've been through with your own drinking.

I definitely have a heightened ability to see other people's dysfunction, and when this happens I can do more to help.

48

Romance: Learning What Real Love Is

TWO MONTHS AFTER GETTING sober, I was introduced to Shelby at a Seahawks game by a coworker trying to uplift my spirits after my divorce. At the time, I wasn't expecting anything serious. I was honestly just looking to have some fun.

But something surprising happened: Shelby and I connected on a deep level that I hadn't experienced before. In my drinking days, I don't think I was capable of that kind of intimacy and vulnerability. I was locked into superficial thinking about relationships.

We instantly clicked and have been together ever since. We've had our ups and downs over the years, but we've grown together. We're committed to acknowledging our flaws, understanding how our upbringings have shaped us, and helping each other become the best versions of ourselves we can be. I've come to see that real love requires collaboration, compromise, and mutual respect—it's not just about fulfilling my own needs.

Shelby has never witnessed my drunken antics firsthand—she's only heard the crazy stories about my escapades. I'm grateful she didn't have to experience that radical behavior from me, and getting sober allowed me to show up as my authentic self in this relationship.

With sobriety has come greater self-awareness about how I was shaped by my childhood experiences. I can recognize emotional triggers that used to provoke irritation—and more drinking—but now I have healthier coping mechanisms.

For example, I used to snap at Shelby for leaving the water running while doing the dishes because it reminded me of my cash-strapped parents' fixation about wasting money.

Thanks to working with a life coach, Shelby and I have open conversations about issues like this that are rooted in our different upbringings. She's become a lot more understanding about my trigger and makes an effort to shut off the water for me. And I'm learning to pause, breathe, and avoid overreacting to situations that aren't relevant to our current reality. We're finding compromises out of love and respect for each other.

My sobriety journey has expanded my perspective on what a loving partnership can be. Instead of the narrow, self-centered view I had before, I'm going much deeper—addressing childhood issues, practicing mindfulness, and collaborating with Shelby in a way that nurtures both of our growth.

49

Sobriety's Financial Upside

THE MOST SURPRISING THING about sobriety was that my career didn't come crashing down without alcohol's liquid crutch to prop things up.

While booze once seemed integral to my financial success, business continued booming after I got sober. It made me wonder if removing that social lubricant and devoting more focus to the actual work all those years could have turbocharged my professional trajectory even more.

No doubt the hundreds of thousands of dollars previously spent accumulating bar tabs could have been better allocated. Sober success turned out to be quite lucrative after kicking a very expensive habit to the curb.

50

You're Different When You're Drunk

AS A SOBER PERSON, it's easy to notice how different people change when they drink. Some people get sloppy and dumb. Others start to tell the same stories over and over. Becoming more aware of these behaviors has given me insights about the best times to make an exit from situations that are only going to get worse.

One of the biggest questions I get is "How do you deal with all the drunken idiots?" It's really kind of simple—you just leave when you recognize the warning signs, such as slurred speech, talking too loud, or losing balance. You start to recognize the patterns in different people's behaviors, and you can graciously excuse yourself before things get out of hand.

I always remind myself that I used to be like that once, and I sure don't miss having to apologize for how dumb or embarrassing I was. I can now channel all the energy I used to expend making up for stupid behavior into much healthier and more productive things. This is a huge motivator to stay sober for the rest of my life.

51

A Willingness to Sacrifice

WHEN A FRIEND OF mine hit rock bottom with his drinking, it was his wife who took the courageous step to get him help. She had sacrificed so much over the years—missing out on social events with friends, tiptoeing around his destructive behavior—all to keep him out of trouble. But she finally reached her limit and called me for support.

I'll never forget the day she dropped her husband off at the Santa Ana airport, entrusting me to get him to rehab safely. I flew in from Seattle and met him in the terminal, where he was slamming down shots at a Mexican restaurant. He drank on the flight back to Seattle, and when we got to my house I knew he wasn't going to stop. So, we went to a bar and I watched him get obliterated out of his eyeballs. Even after we got home, he found some old booze in my garage and drank even more.

He wasn't happy about going to the same place I went to for my aversion therapy, but his wife had given him an ultimatum and he knew it was his last chance with her. They met in college and had a normal partying experience, but alcohol got its hooks in my friend and brought him to the dark side. I was also a bad influence on him over the years, and I was happy to do my part to help him see the light of sobriety.

The next morning he was a complete mess, hung over and emotional. I took him to Schick Shadel Hospital and he broke down in the lobby. "You'll be fine," I told him. "I'll come see you every day."

Because my friend had been drinking the day before his admission, he had to do a three-day detox before they could start him on the Duffy Day/Therapy cycle. He was upset about having to spend the extra time there, but I did what I said I'd do and greeted him with support and encouragement every day, often in the form of motivational books and M&Ms.

Now my friend is doing great and is filled with gratitude for the wife who was his rock through his darkest times. He knows many spouses can't sustain that role as addiction ravages a relationship. But his wife's strength and commitment to repairing their family never wavered. She sacrificed so much—and now it's his turn to reciprocate.

With sobriety came a new perspective. The same social events he once deprived her of attending, he now insists on experiencing together, no longer consumed by selfish impulses. While being around alcohol is still challenging for him at times, he's determined to create new, positive memories without having to take part in every aspect of the festivities.

His willingness to be there for his wife in a new way is a powerful testament that sobriety's ripple effects extend far beyond the individual. When loved ones make profound sacrifices, the act of reciprocating that gift can be the greatest motivation to remain on a positive path.

52

Moving from Influence to Leadership

IN MY DRINKING DAYS, I foolishly thought I was some hot shot, impressing clients and coworkers with my ability to outdrink everyone.

I was delusional, blind to how I was more of a toxic bad influence than an inspirational figure.

While my hard-partying persona attracted a certain rowdy type of customer, it just as easily repelled others. I know for a fact that I missed out on lucrative deals because some clients didn't want to trust their money with a drunken buffoon like me.

But I was successful, and I had a lot of influence in my company. As the haze cleared after I got sober, however, I finally saw what a bad influence I really was. I finally recognized how my cavalier drinking had negatively swayed plenty of team members and associates down destructive paths right alongside me. The reckless antics I once flaunted as "cool" were exposed as the selfish, irresponsible actions of an addict unfit for true leadership.

Today, my influence extends in the complete opposite direction. The people around me operate from a place of health, clarity, and purpose. Instead of encouraging delinquent behavior, I watch over my team members with a nurturing eye, empowering them to uphold professional standards and uplifting them through any personal struggles. My example now motivates others to bring their brightest selves to work each day.

I'll never be able to undo the damaging effects my drinking had on certain people I worked with over the years. But I can make amends by embodying the principled leadership they deserved all along. Through consistency, accountability, and service, I'm driving a cultural renaissance at my company—proving that a sober mindset isn't the death of fun, but the catalyst for maximizing our collective potential.

53

Celebrating Life Without the Buzz

BACK IN APRIL 2016, I achieved a major career milestone by selling my company for a lucrative windfall. When that money hit my account during a trip to Vegas, I went on an even more outrageous bender than usual, fully embodying my "life of the party" persona. Little did I know that just over a year later, in October 2017, I'd commit to a lifetime of sobriety.

At first, I wondered how I'd be able to keep bringing that same electric energy without alcohol as my social lubricant. My entire business was built on a philosophy of entertaining clients and making people feel that contagious motivation to let loose and have an amazing time. Wouldn't giving up drinking make me dull and boring?

Thankfully, those fears proved unfounded. I quickly realized that my ability to create special moments, forge memorable connections, and make others feel happy and inspired had nothing to do with being intoxicated myself. If anything, my sober presence allows me to truly tap into the essence of any celebratory experience without the distorting veil of inebriation.

These days, I still go all-out to uplift spirits and foster an atmosphere of revelry around me—I just don't need alcohol's artificial aid. Every Christmas, I spend around $8,000 treating clients and colleagues to top-shelf liquor, not because I crave it myself, but because I derive genuine joy from gifting others an opportunity to indulge. My sobriety doesn't make me a killjoy—I meet people wherever they are on their journeys, judgment-free.

While my "drunk and disorderly" antics are fortunately relics of the past, I've discovered an even more potent way to get the party started: radiating authentic enthusiasm, zest for life, and gratefulness for human connection. These soulful ingredients create an atmosphere that's much better than any boozy high, and I still get to be the life of the party.

54

Navigating Temptation: Crafting Your Custom Toolkit

MAINTAINING LONG-TERM SOBRIETY requires resilience and strategic navigation through life's temptations. Over the years, I've cultivated a powerful arsenal of practical tools and strategies to safeguard my recovery journey, from building a solid support network to setting clear boundaries around situations that may trigger cravings.

The most effective toolbox is a highly personalized one tailored to your unique temperament and needs. As a classic extrovert, for example, I thrive by keeping myself immersed in social activities. Spending too much time alone can make me restless. My more introverted sober friends, on the other hand, keep their social exposure to a minimum—especially in situations where alcohol is present—as too much stimulation saps their energy.

When it comes to staying on track with a sober lifestyle, some find strength in meditation's quiet solitude, while others prefer the community and vulnerability of an AA meeting. Exploring breath work, journaling, fasting, cold showers, and regular exercise can also provide pathways to self-regulation.

The key is taking an open-minded, experimental approach to discover what rituals resonate. You've lived with yourself this entire journey, so deep down you likely have a good sense of the types of activities that will buoy your spirit and resolve. Don't be afraid to try new solutions until you've assembled a toolkit that feels tailor-made.

I'll be sharing some things that worked for me in the sections below but remember there's no single blueprint, or even a need to conform to someone else's idea of how sobriety should look. Maintaining an alcohol-free existence is an intensely personal undertaking requiring customized care. With some patience and self-compassion, you can forge your own finely tuned set of practices to help you navigate the sober life with grace.

55

The Past Is Past

NO MATTER HOW YOU decide to approach your sobriety, one of the most librating mind-sets to cultivate is the recognition that your past doesn't define who you are today. The person you were while drinking is not the unchange-able truth of your being.

We're all dynamic, everchanging souls, con-stantly shedding old skins and emerging anew through life's ebbs and flows. No matter what unfolds down the road for you—marriage, di-vorce, parenthood, career changes, caring for loved ones—you'll continually outgrow your current self and blossom into new versions.

Lots of people hold onto an identity formed during their darkest, most destructive drinking years—but you don't have to. Just by entertain-ing the idea of a sober lifestyle, you've proven your capacity to evolve beyond who you once were. Let that be a reminder of the growth and reinvention still to come.

With each new sunrise, you can awaken as someone more free, more optimistic, and more fully alive than the day before.

56

My Trusted Tribe

THE CIRCLE OF PEOPLE in my life has shrunk dramatically—almost as much as my beer belly! With no more drunken BBQs at the house or bar lunches that open doors to wild evenings, I don't waste precious time on meaningless relationships anymore.

When I was drinking, I had a circle of more than 25 people I could count on to go booze it up with me whenever I wanted to. When all those people faded away, I was a little scared at first but now the fewer friendships I have are much deeper and I'm a better person because of it.

Lately, outside my immediate family, I've been sticking with my core couples: Ryan and Carolyn, Steve and Diane, Matt and Bunz, and Dane and Amy. Ryan and Steve are sober and the others still drink, but I'd say a bit less so because of us.

These people are the rocket boosters helping me get to the next level in every aspect of my life. I can talk to them about anything, and they can point out my blind spots, like the people Ray Dalio talks about in *Principles for Success*.

I keep my circle close, but I understand that the system is dynamic. Over time, some of your core people might peel off while new people come to help you go even higher. You might have several tight circles of friends in different areas of your life, which may or may not overlap.

The key is surrounding yourself with people who cheer you on and uplift you, while you reciprocate that supportive energy. It's important to recognize that some individuals are natural initiators, while others are more inclined to join in. In my circle, I tend to be the one who gets everyone together and coordinates the details, and it's a role I happily embrace. However, not everyone is wired this way. Rather than taking offense if others don't take the lead, it's wise to understand and appreciate people's inherent natures. The important thing is cultivating a network of positivity and mutual encouragement, regardless of who sparks the inspiration.

The fact that I have close friends who are sober is one of the most powerful ways I stay on course. We're constantly elevating each other, driving one another to perpetually improve our lives.

We talk daily about our ambitions and goals, constantly checking in with each other. If someone's tone hints at turbulence, we provide steadying support. Sharing the sobriety journey has solidified our already profoundly close friendships.

The company you keep charts your present and future trajectory. That's why I work so hard to maintain a vital core inner circle, selectively widening from there. My aspiration? Proximity to individuals I strive to emulate.

I follow successful sober mentors across different domains of life. Some are focused on energy and peak performance, others on mindset and attitude. These inspirational figures fuel my current obsession: continual growth informed by positive influences that benefit me, my kids, my team members, and my friends.

I believe everyone enters our lives for a reason, and I encourage you to honor that truth by embracing each encounter and learning what you need to learn from everybody you meet. But, at the same time, recognize that some connections must be released to allow new growth to occur.

57

Team YOU!

AS YOU NAVIGATE SOBRIETY, it's vital to cultivate a robust support system beyond just friends and family. If you're able to, surround yourself with experts, professionals, and resources attuned to your specific needs and growth goals.

For me, having a fantastic therapist skilled in PTSD work has been invaluable for unpacking deep-rooted issues. My life coach provides motivating accountability to continually step outside my comfort zone and achieve my goals. And working with a relationship coach has helped strengthen the intimate bonds with my partner.

While no amount of counseling can ever fully undo the adverse impacts my addictive behaviors had on my kids and other loved ones, the self-work I've been doing since becoming sober has been paying profound dividends. I'm a better person today because of my commitment to therapy and self-improvement. And the enriched relationships I now have with my children and others close to me are guided by that growth mindset.

The road rises up to greet you when you assemble a "dream team" customized for your personal and emotional evolution. Don't be afraid to explore different approaches—support groups, coaches, counselors, books, videos, podcasts, etc. Introducing new perspectives and practices fosters exponential growth and positive change.

Your sober journey is a precious unfolding, one best undertaken with external guides and resources that illuminate the path alongside your own deepening self-knowledge. Let the experiences of professionals, authors, and peer communities initiate you into higher levels of authenticity and peace.

58

Cultivating Discipline: A Day in the Life

DISCIPLINE BEGINS THE MOMENT my eyes open between 5:00 and 5:30 a.m. Instead of grabbing my phone, I write in my journal for five to 10 minutes, hydrate, do two minutes of breath work, work out, and nourish my body with a nutrient-dense shake. A cold shower follows, providing an invigorating morning reset.

This regimented ritual prepares me for a productive day. By maximizing my morning hours, I set the tone for what's to come. After breakfast, I power through emails, work items, and social media obligations before hitting the road for client visits by 8:30 a.m.

I break for a healthy lunch, then revisit any unfinished tasks with vigorous focus. When I'm in Seattle, I'll often meet my mom or my daughter Maddy for dinner and by 8:30 p.m. I'm winding down, reading for a bit before lights out.

This discipline keeps me out of trouble and directs my energy for maximum productivity. It's a lifestyle that requires mental fortitude, but it yields tremendous fulfillment.

59

Gratitude: A Cornerstone Practice

MY MORNING ROUTINE BEGINS with a few grounding breaths and a gratitude practice. I mentally walk through the abundant blessings in my life, including my family, friends, health, work, etc.

This intentional gratitude keeps me focused on the good that's already present in my life, rather than what's lacking. It centers me in a contented mindset before proceeding with the rest of my disciplined morning.

Feeling grateful gives me more energy for the mental and physical demands of my regimented lifestyle. When you appreciate blessings like mobility, mental clarity, and access to good food and loving friends, relatives, and co-workers, you no longer have any excuses for not striving to reach your full potential.

A gratitude practice combats entitlement and restores humility about the life I've rebuilt in sobriety. Gratitude also makes it harder to play the victim.

By beginning every morning centered in appreciative awareness, I cultivate fertile ground for the rest of the day's disciplines to take root and thrive.

60

Get Grounded

ANOTHER HELPFUL THING I do is incorporate grounding rituals into my daily discipline.

This includes spending time walking barefoot on cold grass or earth whenever possible and using a pulsed electromagnetic field (PEMF) mat when I don't have the luxury of outdoor time.

The PEMF mat helps harmonize my body's natural electromagnetic frequencies that can become disrupted by environmental stressors. Twenty minutes a day leaves me feeling revitalized and more centered.

When I'm in Seattle, I make a point to get outside and go completely barefoot on the lawn or garden beds, allowing the crisp blades of grass and cool soil to reinvigorate my physical connection to the planet and the present moment. This tactile grounding relieves any mental haziness I might start to experience during the day.

These practices are simple but profound ways to heighten mind-body awareness and combat the alienation of modern life's ubiquitous shoes, screens, and disconnection from nature. By quite literally rooting into the here-and-now through ancient grounding techniques, I fortify my resilience and reduce energetic stagnation.

Combining gratitude with these grounding rituals monumentally enhances my body's ability to operate at peak levels. I remain centered and relaxed, avoiding the temptation to disconnect among anxious, swirling thoughts.

61

Doing the Math: Sobriety's Cost-Benefit Analysis

ADJUSTING TO YOUR AUTHENTIC sober self and navigating life's challenges without alcohol as a crutch can take some getting used to. Some people struggle with losing their social lubricant or excuse for inappropriate behavior. Others take to sobriety like a duck to water from the start.

The differentiating factor often comes down to how much you still romanticize and crave the perceived enjoyment of drinking or get caught up in the dreaded fear of missing out. It's easy to wallow in self-pity, thinking "Why can't I have that beautiful glass of wine? Everyone else can indulge, why not me?"

But that's when you must get honest with yourself through a clear-eyed cost-benefit analysis of alcohol's role in your life. If you're being real, the gifts of not partaking should quickly outweigh whatever fleeting "fun" you associated with having a drink in your hand. The positives you can genuinely attribute to alcohol will likely be very few.

For me, the biggest benefit of not drinking has been regaining my time. Instead of wasting hours in a bar, I go for hikes, bond with my kids, and enrich myself with great books. I didn't grasp how much of a time-suck drinking was until long after I quit.

A sober friend of mine still experiences vivid drinking dreams in which he knows he shouldn't imbibe but he does it anyway, often with his wife looking on in disapproval. While these dreams are disorienting, they show how ingrained the alcoholic mindset can be and the constant vigilance required to combat it. When my friend awakens, grateful the dream wasn't real, his motivation is reinvigorated.

The truth is, you don't need alcohol to celebrate success or numb your pain—those are false justifications the alcoholic mind learns to lean on. The healthier path is to discover new rhythms, rituals, and coping mechanisms in your alcohol-free life that provide genuine fulfillment and solace.

Keep in mind that rewiring habitual patterns takes discipline and persistence. It's a gradual process marked by many small victories before new ways of doing things take hold. But eventually, with consistent effort, you'll find new sources of fun and fulfillment.

When you do the honest math, the scales always tip heavily in favor of eliminating alcohol's negative costs on your health, relationships, finances, and sense of self. Sobriety's gifts of clarity, presence, and reclaimed time are invaluable.

62

Power of the Pause: Mastering Your Thoughts

WHEN YOU EXPERIENCE TURBULENT emotions or cravings, it's important to pause and breathe before acting on your impulses. Thoughts aren't actions, but the decisions you make when urges arise can dictate the entire trajectory of your life.

Practice box breathing—inhale for four counts, hold for four counts, exhale for four counts, and hold for four counts. This simple technique helps center you in the present moment, allowing you to feel the calm clarity sobriety brings. Even when engulfed by difficult situations, remind yourself how much worse it would feel layering a hangover or drunken haze on top of it all.

When those intrusive, nagging thoughts try to derail your progress, stare them down. Recognize them as mere noise from the ego, not reality. The mind is a busy place—we have a staggering 75,000 thoughts per day according to Ed Mylett, with 91% of them being recycled from the day before. But you have the power to take control of the transformative 9%.

By pausing to breathe and reframe negative self-talk, you assert mastery over your mindset. The urge to drink loses its grip when you can clearly see the upward spiral sobriety provides, including feelings of accomplishment, gratitude for clear mornings, and authentic presence with loved ones.

The split-second decisions made when cravings strike hold immense power. Pause, breathe, and reconnect with your "why" for pursuing a better life. In that space of mindfulness, the wiser choice becomes clear. Master your thoughts, and you master the direction of your journey.

63

Sober Socializing Hacks

WHEN YOU FIND YOURSELF in social settings where alcohol is flowing, it can be challenging to resist cravings and avoid feeling like an outsider. But with a few creative sober socializing hacks, you can stay connected to the celebratory vibes without compromising your alcohol-free lifestyle.

For some, ordering a fancy mocktail or virgin cocktail is the perfect way to mirror the drinking experience while still abstaining. Sipping on a zingy non-alcoholic mojito or a refreshing cucumber cooler helps you feel involved in the festivities and takes away pressure to fit in by drinking.

If mocktails don't appeal to you, or if they aren't an option at a given location, get crafty with soda water and garnishes. A club soda with a lime wedge or splash of cranberry juice in a rocks glass has a sophisticated look that blends right in. You can even request it without a straw to mimic the casual sipping of a cocktail.

Wherever the party goes, you don't owe anyone an explanation for your choices. Your sobriety is a personal journey, so avoid calling excessive attention to yourself unless you're comfortable doing so. With a bit of situational awareness, you can fully participate in social affairs while prioritizing your well-being.

Of course, the true sober socializing hack is cultivating an unshakeable mindset of gratitude and self-assurance. When you're grounded in the conviction that your sober presence is an invaluable gift to yourself and others, staying focused on the shared experience rather than what's in everyone's glasses becomes a lot less difficult. Sobriety is nothing to be self-conscious about, but a profound source of clarity, joy, and connection to be celebrated alongside any other milestone.

64

Tap into Spiritual Power

A SPIRITUAL PRACTICE CAN provide an anchor of peace and clarity. Prayer, meditation, and other techniques can keep you centered and aware of the mindset needed to stay on the path of successful sobriety.

For some, it's surrendering to a higher power, like my friend who recites:

> *"God, help me be strong. Prevent*
> *dark thoughts and actions from*
> *entering my head and heart.*
>
> *Help me avoid self-pity.*
> *Guide me to live authentically and treat*
> *my loved ones with the care they deserve.*
>
> *Remind me to breathe and*
> *pause when I feel lost."*

For others, it's a plea for daily reminders of life's beauty:

> *"God, show me your presence*
> *in nature, my children, and*
> *the goodness around me.*
>
> *Reassure me that I can live*
> *fully without alcohol.*
>
> *When I'm selfish or pitying*
> *myself, steer me right.*
>
> *Help me love my wife so*
> *she feels peaceful.*
>
> *Let me see the unique gift*
> *in each of my kids.*

*Make me a kind, positive
influence wherever I go.*

Give me purpose beyond myself.

Quiet the obsession over drinking."

My own ritual is a simple ask for protection and a call to service:

*"Lord, keep my Bailey, Maddy, Emerson,
the rest of my family, and closest friends
happy, healthy, and safe.*

*Provide guidance to positively impact
everyone I encounter."*

Whatever way you conceptualize it, inviting spiritual energy into your sobriety journey can be profoundly grounding. By accessing a higher power, wisdom, or intention beyond your own willpower, you eliminate the constant need for control. Life's beauty reveals itself more vividly. Dark thoughts lose their grip.

In the sacred pause of prayer and meditation, you reroute from the relentless mental churn onto a path of peace and purpose. Spiritual practices are a way to recharge with the intention and motivation to embrace an authentic, alcohol-free existence, one breath, one step, and one day at a time.

65

Forgive Yourself

ONE OF THE MOST vital lessons I've learned on my wild ride to sobriety is the importance of forgiving yourself when life inevitably knocks you down. It's not about avoiding the hits altogether—that's impossible. The key is having the resilience and self-compassion to keep getting back up after taking a punch.

This mindset reminds me of the ethos in boxing—you don't lose the fight when you get knocked down, you lose when you don't keep fighting. The most successful boxers understand they'll get hit hard at times. What separates them is their ability to reset, recalibrate, and see the next round as a fresh start.

Like the metaphor of boxing, life will keep throwing haymakers our way: setbacks, disappointments, losses, mistakes, and unanticipated challenges that drop us squarely on the mat. In those moments, we can't recoil in fear or self-loathing over the hit itself. That only diminishes our ability to rebound.

Instead, we must practice forgiving ourselves for getting rocked, while resolving to rise again with poise and determination. It's okay to take a moment to let the sting subside. But then we dust ourselves off, dispensing with useless shame or rumination.

Forgiving ourselves is the ultimate show of resilience—a reclamation of our self-worth which restores the stamina to weather whatever comes next. It's the mental conditioning for perseverance through the infinite rounds that forge our legacy.

66

Make it Great

THESE DAYS, MY DRIVING goal is to make a positive impact on everyone I meet. I want to help empower people to create great lives for themselves and spread that positivity outward. It's an expansive mission.

My parents, especially my mom, instilled this giving mindset in me from a young age. They taught me that just one meaningful relationship can completely transform your life's trajectory for the better.

A significant portion of my time, around 30%, is now devoted to helping others however I can, through coaching, mentoring, and leading by example. At work alone, 364 people have direct access to me. I think people feel comfortable talking with me because I'm just a regular guy who overcame alcoholism's grip. If I can do it, anyone else can with the right mindset and support system in place.

I always emphasize to those I counsel that while I'll do everything possible to guide and support them, they're ultimately responsible for their own lives and choices. It's the hard truth I often have to remind myself of as well. You can't just look to others to create the change you want—whether it's becoming sober, creating a better relationship, finding a better job, or any other situation. Taking radical responsibility is key: The next time you have a dream or goal you want to pursue, tell yourself "It's on me to make it great."

Don't be afraid to break down your ambitions into incremental steps and start small. Over time, with consistency, little steps can compound into great achievements. As I told you before, it took me many months to build up the willpower to stay under an ice-cold shower for three minutes straight, but I got there by adding just a few more seconds each day.

The key is gaining clarity on what you're trying to accomplish, then reverse-engineering a routine to get you there, piece by piece. Schedule supporting actions like workouts, meditation sessions, or mentor meetings in your calendar. When you inevitably face setbacks, learn from the experience, adjust your approach, and keep pushing forward with resilience.

Making your life great can start today, and it can continue as a day-by-day process of productive habits. You have full control over undertaking a journey of positive change, one mindful choice at a time.

I wish you the best of luck, and I'm always happy to provide an ear or additional guidance. Feel free to reach out to me anytime at ian@wildridetosobriety.com.

Acknowledgments

THIS BOOK WAS A long time coming—especially if you count my drinking years. I have many people to thank, and apologize to, for their role in its creation.

First, a huge hug to my three kids—Bailey, Maddy, and Emerson. You endured so much growing up with an alcoholic father, yet you still gift me with loving counsel today. I treasure your generous contributions to this book, knowing you could have really ripped me apart if you wanted to. I love you to the moon and back.

Next, I owe a profound debt of gratitude to two of my best friends, Ryan and Steve. We were a hard-partying trio in our early career days, somehow surviving innumerable boozy "business trips" and happy hours. While I was the first to finally walk the sobriety path once and for all, it's great to share this journey with you both now. Your constant candor and encouragement make me a better man.

Rounding out my closest circle are my other ride-or-dies, Dane and Amy, Matt and Bunz, Ryan's wife Carolyn, and Steve's wife Diane. I love that no topic is off limits among us. Thank you for the nudges to keep improving myself—such as finishing this book—and for the unwavering love and support you've shown through years of great times, both drunk and sober. I can't thank my closest circle enough—I love you!

My love, Shelby, has been a constant source of support, even though she's remarkably never witnessed my drinking firsthand. Thank you, Shelby, for consistently nurturing our growth together and cheering me on. Your loving presence made this book possible.

I'd also like to express my gratitude to Mike, Lori, Joel, Julie, T-Free, Zack, Michelle, Anthony, Malisa, Jim, Ginger, Nancy, and Tim.

My life coach Angie (angie@geardup.biz) and my relationship coach Christina (Instagram: @therelationshipboss) have both been instrumental in keeping me on the path towards physical health and mental clarity. I deeply appreciate your love and support, and your continued guidance along my wild ride!

Naturally, I want to thank my parents for giving me booze and cigarettes from the time I started walking—if it wasn't for you, I'd never have such a wonderful book cover! In all seriousness, you both gave me a zest for life that makes every day a good time. It turns out, you don't even need alcohol!

I want to thank my brothers—Derick, Bruce, and Allan—for their support. They all know that once the journey starts, it's forever.

I also want to express my gratitude to Gregory Thybulle, whose random gym conversation provided a referral to writer Ed Sweet. Ed capably helped mold my stories into this cohesive narrative. I'm grateful for his guidance through the writing process and I look forward to a lifelong friendship. Without you, Ed, I couldn't have told my story—thank you for bringing it to life.

And lastly, I want to thank David, Manon, Kerri, and the whole team at AuthorImprints for their design and production expertise. Thanks to their creativity and attention to detail, this book is something I'm proud to have people hold in their hands and take to heart.

About the Author

IAN FEE'S LIFE HAS been a whirlwind journey, from his roots in New Westminster, BC to the peaks of the hotel industry and an eventual foray into the automotive world. Born with an insatiable drive, Ian spent his formative years in Bellingham, WA until his family's relocation to The Salton Sea, California at age 12.

After graduating high school in 1990, Ian's entrepreneurial spirit manifested in the fast-paced world of hotel management. By 1992, he had completed a vocational program at Century Business College while juggling shifts at a Holiday Inn in San Diego. Ian's tenacity earned him a coveted position that same year at the prestigious Embassy Suites in Bellevue, WA.

A rising star, Ian swiftly climbed the ranks to Assistant General Manager at Embassy Suites. His multifaceted role included overseeing night operations, bar and banquet management, sales, marketing, engineering, and the iconic Pahrump's Nightclub. 1994 brought another opportunity as he spearheaded the opening of a new property in Temecula, California.

1995 marked a defining personal milestone as Ian and his wife Nicole welcomed their first child, son Bailey. Seeking to be closer to family, they requested a transfer back to Seattle, where daughter Madison was born in 1997. Despite the demands of his blossoming career, Ian's enterprising nature kicked in and he launched a landscaping business in his downtime.

In 2000, Ian traded hotels for cars, accepting a Finance Manager position at Frontier Chevrolet, followed by a similar stint at Sims Honda. In 2002, he co-founded a dealership marketing company with two partners. The venture proved so successful that it was acquired by Southwest Dealer Services in 2016. 2010 brought another joyful addition with the birth of youngest daughter Emerson.

Today, Ian serves as Market VP of Sales at Acrisure Protection Group, overseeing teams across multiple regions. His dedication, discipline, and determination have propelled him from modest beginnings to the pinnacles of success in multiple industries. Through it all, Ian's commitment to personal growth and family has provided the solid foundation for a life well-lived.

Feel free to contact me!

Instagram: @ian.fee
@makeitgreat.me
Facebook: Ian Fee make it great
Tiktok: @ianfeemig
Email: ian@wildridetosobriety.com
Cell: (206) 571-3068